Dedication

We are bringing a new light to the era in which we live. May this scroll be translated for your understanding, whoever you are! We always live with less when we are spiritually blessed. We can help to end oppression in all parts of the world

Boosting Confidence

Removing complacency, stopping the psychological and sociological problems of people with spiritual skills, that can help do this for you to cut through the red tape of reality that causes red bloodshed.

This information is here in hopes that I can inspire others that may bring knowledge we can share will add to what will be given to you and you alone that will add up to the divine order of your life's journey with the quickening that multiply to increase your blessings to the fullness of the message of or with righteousness by the creator of life.

There is new work that is waiting to be released and a move that is being written to bring about a better way of living and thinking to the world we live in thanks to God.

I can only say I will give it my all to keep it on the straight and narrow as I write the words that come to me from the Holy Spirit that will conform you and strengthen you in all hours of the day and night.

I have foretold of many things in my quest to give you the truth of the gospel in a way of my best understanding as a trailblazer of the messages I have learned about. I have seen the darkness of the worldliness in a presence and I will say that gave me enough light to see at times when I thought it was no light to see thanks to the Lord. Therefore I implore you in the name of the Lord to put the bits and pieces of what I have written together and it may need to be known by you so it can fit into your life.

This book is unauthorized by anyone whose name is mentioned, but the author.

This information will help lead you to the keys to freedom which opens the door to the light that guides you away from the dark side of life, where the beastly presences are that enslave and have control over people.

Definitions

Tyrannosaur - a large fierce flesh-eating dinosaur that walked on powerful hind legs and had small forelegs. It lived during the Cretaceous Period and was the largest carnivore.

Tyranny - cruel use of power: cruelty and injustice in the exercise of power or authority over others; oppressive government by one or more people who exercise absolute power cruelly and unjustly

Tyrant - absolute ruler: an absolute ruler who exercises power cruelly and unjustly. Authoritarian person: an unjust and oppressive exerciser of authority

Tyrant plus rhino = a two in one pack that can cause death.

Tyranny must know they have recompense to live by. How do we do this? Through the heart by making them recognize hate at first and reverse the way they think. This is the beginning of the work that is planned to bless the world phase I phase II is under construction. Date will be disclosed to anyone involved in this project. Thank you

Does this have an ungodly effect on some? Yes

The power of darkness that does not want you to see the light can draw or pull you in.

Then Towerism Came Along

They say beauty killed the beast, so let's use ugliness to wake up the conscience that is dead to bring life where there is none. This can be done on an individual basis as if we are God's mission impossible team.

We are talking about one who displays prehistoric traits within the mindset and heart. How can they be helped to fix that state of existence?

What must be done to stop towerism around the world? We must know that the demons in towers have weaknesses. We can stop them but first we must know who they are and that is a problem since there are lots of people who act like they know but really don't know.

The incredible thing I can say I witness is the towerism in people when it doesn't need a hint to come down. It is timely that gives my heart cheers and they know not what they did but reward truth to change. It does bless the Lord.

Know that you have no sealed sell to hell when the Lord is involved. All things will pass when they come into the fruition of fruitfulness with the Lord because a miracle takes place to be witnessed by all.

This book will teach people how to navigate through any of the storms and rough times that can be placed on the people's doorstep by a leader to see the daylight to come into view that helps to create peace through the foresight it gives you a chance to receive.

Yes you can determine the state of what can be present in the land you love by way of the atmosphere. It starts inside of you and it can overflow outside of you with enough people believing in faith without violence.

As people who belong to any nation of the world can control, we can control our environment with the spiritual skills that we make present that can govern over the person or people who are governing our nation with the use of our prayers.

The books all are some kind of spiritual health process that tries to do better than sub for a teacher the words let you become a teacher.

The process of seeing if people can put the world back up on its feet again may seem grandiose. It would remove a big disease and replace it with love.

The ending of towerism can give people a renewed way of thinking and living. If we can create a simultaneous positive response with the world it can take the edge off of people emotionally and relieve stress on a spiritual level of thinking.

This is a part of history that has been written into our life before we became a part of this life. It has just come into fruition for all to know what they have not known before to save people who are intertwined in the web of a kind of deceitfulness that may not have been believed in the past.

Pollination time has come to release the sweet fragrance of this flower of life to revive the senses of the people.

The Real Deal is
People Have to Learn to Repurpose Themselves

To keep up with their right state of mind in their life there are too many old stigmas people attach themselves to that hang on to them that are harmful that must be let go to make room for new growth because when you do not feed the brain matter on the spiritual level, it gets gobbled up within the material presence that fails to increase its foresight about the development of love. Without that, it is not healthy.

With a leader, if They want to really do the right thing for the world and not just himself and acquaintances we the people have to lead him there to a new state of existence he must learn to adapt to and repurpose himself with. It is no illusion, but it is a consequence in the name of Jesus. Therefore believe it and receive it.

A pathway to stop any kind of dictatorship and towerism that has so many leaders of smaller nations from hoarding the funds that add up to billions that can be released in order to help the people who are living in poverty and distress because of the lack of healthcare, etc. So they can join with the rest of the world in increasing a godly global balance.

For The People

If you can become better than content you and I if we use the power of the spiritual intervention that we have been endowed with by the creator plus putting a togetherness as a body of believers this can change the way a man thinks so he will not continue to believe in his principles of thought by or from the righteousness that can be placed upon him by way of the Lord's guaranteeing the wishes of the people as if we were in a fight with a group of people and they did not want to do as the Lord wishes before we could present this dilemma that the Lord can clear up and free them from destroying themselves but this is not the case and no one wants to stay in the belly of a whale.

To the Government of Every Nation

If you want to know how to make whatever land you live in, this is the way to go first says the Lord. Can we take this lead that is the question we must know in our hearts first of all starting at the top to work our way down.

Our objective to live with ourselves should be to share holiness openly, earnestly and reverently. The meaning of this is to use the shower power to cleanse one's self.

The truth is we are to renew a part of our history daily in our lives as a race of people. we are to improve the stability as much as we can. It is to make us more able to show each other that we are the superior being that has been created to bring love to the existence of mankind.

That is right, we are more than special we are made from love but as we know it has been tainted by Satan and he tries to delude it as much as possible and discredit it to stop it from growing. This is why we

7

have to show we can live above this evil doing thing that is in our presence.

Now the truth will set you free but the blindness to truth can't be seen by the unbeliever that is the problem the whole world over and the untruth has brought so much harm to people that it makes some even fear the truth.

Know the process of the arrows started in the U.S.A., but it can have the same affect wherever you are.

Now what is or what may be the fore longed conclusion to the process of the prayers that are attached to the arrows? It could be a way to help free people who are stuck in the towers who have towerism all over the world. If we can live in a manner in which we have belief in fairytales in our minds and in our hearts, then why not in our spiritual presence that has a way to outgrow the enemy within one's own mind and soul.

Therefore, if we believe and have faith in the love we are given by the Lord we can see the truth in all things in an order that makes sense, such as if we the people have enough faith that the invisible arrows will reach their destination and perform their duties with the fervency of a spirit in flying up to the heavenly place to be known as gifts. Then we can see and feel the return on what God has given us to share. To not get ahead of myself but it makes me feel excited overwhelmed that what goes up in a way of prayers must come down.

Now what can we look forward to as the arrows fall back down to earth? I think it is the help that will be produced by the different kinds of stairways for the people who need to climb out of the ruts of insecurities in ways that only God may know of right now.

At the same time, we can look forward to seeing the people who we know that are sitting in high places to come down off of their so called high horses to take the stairway down from their power trip that has tripped them up into a zone called towerism and that is more than enough for the fact of once they come down the people go up because the love of the control of self is reinstated to know not to do the wrong by taking or stealing from the people who you may be in power to assist in ending poverty.

Furthermore, in the grand scheme of things this is not just for America it is for the world at large. This means all of the people, none excluded. This movement is not of mankind it is of and about the Lord. it is a part of his plan to end the unwise of the stewards of the world and free them from the traps that have been set upon them from Satan using the greed and selfishness they have fallen prey to out of their blindness to see how to know and show love to the people who may be in need of their guidance

Therefore, we can look forward to helping create a better world regardless of what some may think about what we may be facing. We as people take on this challenge to know that the strength we share has no boundary that limits us when we stand up for the right things we will not fall down for anything wrong.

As the people of one of the greatest countries on the earth we have helped and been a beacon of hope for millions around the world. It is time that we get the blessings back that we have put out by the billions amen. We need to believe in the "what goes out comes back in" principles one turn deserves another.

Time to create some history
for the world that everyone will love.

When something steals your spirit like money or a kind of power that acts like you are too great for your own good; meaning others. It could become deadly in the long run!

Help is Here

To help you stop the crimes against self and humanity, you have to learn what your beliefs are and ways of life that are not right and change them.

There are traditions that may go back 1,000 years that you know of that could have been needed at one time in your ancestors' lives that have no need to be used in the new state of life the fact that change may not be welcome in all ways can be understood but the power of reasoning has to be developed to bring the new and better concepts of life together for all people. This is not just an idea of one phase of life but the second phase of life that gives even the tyrant an opportunity to have a place in heaven that will be of greatness on a scale that supersedes the norm.

This can become a reality if the heart of the beast in this kind of person has the dance of a thousand or more pricks get to them also; in the name of Jesus!

You can steal time and money from yourself if you

don't know how to use it right know matter how much of it you have, especially if it doesn't belong to you in the first place also if you don't learn to accept the light and you can become your own victim of a crime that you commit against yourself by not accepting the truth. People take the truth as a sign of weakness when looking into the light at others that may have the truth within them that shines and the dark sparkle that people see in themselves keeps them on the losing team known as the team of me, myself and I, instead of with the team of the Father, Son, Holy Spirit and for you.

It is time to get the twilight right because some people get lost between the day and night like wrong from right. But not the spirit of people that carry the best part of life throughout life who may have been lost but always tried to find what the true love of Jesus Christ does for everyone.

Big Ups

There is only one level that can put anyone on the spiritual skyway in the place which was created by the Lord and Savior from passing on beyond the earthly death to the heavenly ascension as was with Christ when he left the cross that blessed us and maybe this may be that one road for you and all children of the Lord.

This Part Is Dedicated To That Easter Sunday

In remembrance of the day of true freedom that the Lord has made and called resurrection, that created in part the dunemous spirit; hallelujah. A day that death dies and no longer took life and mountains of troubles became molehills and Satan lost the fight once and for all with all mankind.

Satan's Greatest Tool

To not reveal Satan's greatest tool, that has caused mankind the biggest falls, would be a shame and I have no shame to share only truth.

What is this tool? It is the lack of, misuse of, mistrust of, not sharing of, not knowing what to do with it, the blinding part of, the misrepresentation of, the avoidance of, the don't want to believe in it and the unknown fear of, love. Satan's best tool to make this world as bad as he can make it, comes from the way he tricks us to see love that the Lord died for and the power it gives us.

Now if you say how can that be? I will say look around you and see what the love factors have done wrong that could or should have not been done that way. Now let's fix that by not looking back again because we can look forward with the new way of thinking of how much better we now have a chance to know love and how it works for us without Satan taking it to the level of having it work against us.

We first of all try to learn to love someone by instincts in life; our guardians/parents then others. Now could this be somewhat backward? If so, then what can we do about it. How do we teach our children to love the lord first before us? I can't say at this time but we can at least let them know who is first in their life and it isn't them or us.

Out of this was there was only one person that came

out of their mother's womb that loved the Lord first before they love another?

What is the real point I am making? We are not making it plain enough to ourselves. I am first to know that I must work on the one fact that could never be and that is trying to develop my spirit with a sense of a likeness of one with an even yoke to the love I have in me to be shared with my fellow man as if I had the same state of agape love as the Lord did.

If this level could become as close to us as God wanted, then Satan's tools will be no more in our lives. That will create the evenness of sharing the love the Lord wants us to have that defeats the devil.

The worse enemy of mankind is the thought process of no love that carries and displays this in their lifestyle more than any other culture the natives of the third world countries. They gave in to the life they came out of by way of primitive ways on the level of survival of the fittest along with self-preservation and for most if necessary (cannibalism) on the primitive level.

To make this a many saga in history, the mindset of the people didn't develop as was in modern culture it rescinded into the past to resist the new principles of modern civilization. This was because of the black side of the leaders is on this level being set in their ways. Now what can be done to give their thought pattern a reverse polarity that turns it back in time and bring it forward at the same time God knows and with the right prayers we can learn this to be shared along with the dance; amen!

Dance Sponsored By God Hosted By Bro. Tracy Bush

Now that the prom is over on this newly found dance that lasts a lifetime or more, one question is how do you feel about the world? It is not as important right now how they feel about you as it is how you feel about them. Because they (or the world) will feel the same way about you as you feel about them in general is it like that. Now the dance goes on and on. But the real threat is how many dances will you create in (or for) the people of the world? This is a "them-you" effect of strengthening the emotional bond in the right ways in life between each other, at the same time keeping the dance going and the right kind of emotions flowing.

The Greatest Key to Growth Can Be Yours

If we equate our life with one thing right now whether we are going into or are into or are coming out of a storm we can get things fixed in the fullest capacity.

The words that we can try to say we can do with the reality we live with our faith such as if we need rehabilitation on a certain level that requires a rebirth of the life someone has to renew the mind, body and spirit if we could look at it with the heart with the power that love gives us it could take less than we probably would ever imagine. This can become a reality if you know the love that is contained inside your spirit in connection with the love that was given to you on the day of resurrection of our lord and savior Jesus Christ.

The power to be free from all ungodliness and legends of doom was placed in your heart, through the birth of the level of agape love that very few can place upon their life because the lack of love on such a high level can now reach that present of thought in faith where the Lord was on that day, they can be free.

Time Out, Off, On And In

People have stop too much and need to start taking time out for the enjoyment of a lot more of heaven on earth treatments for our/themselves and family life.

Get Your Recompense

What time is it? It is time for recompense to get back the things that make up the love that some of us never had. I mean before the fall of Adam the love factor was the greatest after the fall there was something that was lost between mankind and God until the Son came to fulfill the prophecy again so mankind can have it all once again if he learned the wisdom of what it takes to receive it for himself.

The recompense is the things that make people whole and full of joy. The thing that is priceless that money can't buy that makes people feel good about each other.

The things that are a part of the missing pieces that can be found in the life we are to be living. But we need the wisdom of the Lord to see what is missing and not there because we put other things in place that may make us feel good but it will not fix a person and make them whole and that causes them to miss out on some holiness in their life.

Noting: No Religion Needed
Only a relationship with the Lord

The unity of family and the level of understanding the reasoning of one another in order not to make war because of the dark side of what was placed around mankind because of the fall of the warring angels from heaven. Do your homework.

A Key to Freedom

Have you ever thought that each day we are getting up to give witness to tell about the resurrection of the Lord? To lock ourselves up out of the unknown side of not in the thing called darkness by the points of light the lord provides to prick the heart continuously.

Get the message out of what the riches have done to the people. Let them know that by not sharing has caused the greed of Solomon.

That is or Needs to be Broken
Before Death Not After Your Death

Flying Is a Must

Now to get to the skyway that leads to the highway you have to crawl before you walk. To do it all stay humble and don't stumble unless it is upward.

While putting this book of no lies together and the information on what it is about in a format on both levels, it gave me understanding of the haves and haves not.

Oh what a plan – let's keep it real now who would not

like to be a part of that team and plan no fuss no must no one getting hurt.

What a way to go into heaven's gates one day with a resume that said I helped rid the world of some of the people like Edi Amin's kind of people.

I myself don't take pride in anyone that has not known true freedom and fall on the behalf of their belief. That is why it is the desire of my heart to teach the way out of darkness to all mankind at whatever stage of life whether it is thinking they may be right or not. The tyrants are just the people because if you can teach a great leader to become a greater leader it is a good thing.

Ezekiel 33:7-20
7. So thou, O son of man, I have set thee a watchman unto the house of Israel; therefore thou shalt hear the word at my mouth, and warn them from me.
8. When I say unto the wicked, O wicked man, thou shalt surely die; if thou dost not speak to warn the wicked from his way, that wicked man shall die in his iniquity; but his blood will I require at thine hand.
9. Nevertheless, if thou warn the wicked of his way to turn from it; if he do not turn from his way, he shall die in his iniquity; but thou hast delivered thy soul.
10. Therefore, O thou son of man, speak unto the house of Israel; Thus ye speak, saying, If our transgressions and our sins be upon us, and we pine away in them, how should we then live?
11. Say unto them, As I live, saith the Lord God, I have no pleasure in the death of the wicked; but that the wicked turn from his way and live: turn ye, turn ye from your evil ways; for why will ye die, O house of

Israel?

12. Therefore, thou son of man, say unto the children of thy people, The righteousness of the righteous shall not deliver him in the day of his transgression: as for the wickedness of the wicked, he shall not fall thereby in the day that he turneth from his wickedness; neither shall the righteous be able to live for his righteousness in the day that he sinneth.

13. When I shall say to the righteous, that he shall surely live; if he trust to his own righteousness, and commit iniquity, all his righteousnesses shall not be remembered; but for his iniquity that he hath committed, he shall die for it.

14. Again, when I say unto the wicked, Thou shalt surely die; if he turn from his sin, and do that which is lawful and right;

15. If the wicked restore the pledge, give again that he had robbed, walk in the statutes of life, without committing iniquity; he shall surely live, he shall not die.

16. None of his sins that he hath committed shall be mentioned unto him: he hath done that which is lawful and right; he shall surely live.

17. Yet the children of thy people say, The way of the Lord is not equal: but as for them, their way is not equal.

18. When the righteous turneth from his righteousness, and committeth iniquity, he shall even die thereby.

19. But if the wicked turn from his wickedness, and do that which is lawful and right, he shall live thereby.

20. Yet ye say, The way of the Lord is not equal. O ye house of Israel, I will judge you every one after his ways.

The main goal is to stop all levels of dictatorship and

anyone who leads the body of people with torment. Our number one goal is, to make ourselves helpful and not offend anyone nor do we ever want to be looked upon as a trouble maker out of the USA and all other countries in the world.

There are at least upwards of 50 plus nations that have dictators, tyrants or oppressive leaders.

At BTHPM, we serve you up a vision with education and wisdom of the Lord that include the wisdom in more book that are available to you.

If there was one that caused the temporary harm to a nation, there may be 20 that will want to replace the loss we have felt by way of their stronger muscle, the heart, because of it being strengthened the right ways.

The people who get trapped in a towerist state have a fever for Solomon's riches. The blind side of this reality that can be fixed by knowing what kind of problem you have, then admitting to it and giving it to the lord to relieve you from it, along with applying a new process of thinking and doing with the where you go and what you do exercises B.K.A. therapy thoughts that keep action thoughts in line to do the right things with the blessings of god on your side and not working against you for a change amen.

What is rhino-ism? Wanting to bully and run over others and let people know don't get in your way; being in control of space that may or may not belong to you. The list goes on and on. I don't want to give ideas.

First of all it is not my need to fulfill an anxiety or a desire to change anyone's faith or belief and religious preference. It is the furthest from my thoughts. Though I can say it is the health of the wisdom I am after to grow it with truth and understanding in more ways than one.

Time to know one of the greatest things in life is, knowing we can love completely without understanding.

I am not writing directly about religion or to persuade anyone about how to think or change someone's beliefs. I am writing to share the wisdom that I have found that creates success when applied by using faith, spirituality and keys that prick the heart.

There is a fact that my spirituality has a place in modern culture that others have applied to their existence for over 2,000 years. This I pronounce as my belief and I do take my teachings from there but don't attempt to persuade anyone to follow my lead just give yourself an open mind to understand what I am presenting to you along with the use of the scripture out of the Holy Bible.

We do this with the answers that is contained in the plan that God gives us that creates his intervention that has an invention that works as you are part of this plan it is as simple as that; spiritual recreation to develop spiritual re-creation that makes something new to use that are older than us.

If you think this is crazy also. What do I have to say to that don't be like the people who thought my Lord and savior was crazy Jesus. This is not a fact finding mission. It is the calling of the wisdom of God to be given and used to help preserve humanity.

I like to think of my work as if on the level of hope when he asked the lord not to destroy a place until he saw if he could get at least one more soul to join the body of Christ to go to heaven.

This falls in line with the ministry work I am trying to do in the third world countries. I know it takes a fishing line that has an endless amount of strings on it to do this but. If the Lord truly supplies the strings all I am required to do is provide the pole and that is my faith in the name of Jesus.

This is what my life's work means to my fellow man that are in need of the answers to the questions they have not considered or figured out that is why we offer a step at a time that can get you where you are in need of going. It is my belief and faith that gives me comfort in knowing how to ask someone of themselves that bring turmoil and trouble to their life on a large scale to look in the mirror to begin to see yourself changing. This I can't say for sure that I have all the right answers about helping but I know it is a part of the work I must complete that takes the new ways of thinking around the world to be placed on the doorstep of people that some call tyrants and dictators and those that have an ungodly spirit that have not yet found a true way of life in their heart for the people they rule over. Now it is not of my plan to do anything that can bring harm to myself or others but the Lord has given me in a part of my in structure to develop the news and let the Holy Spirit do the rest.

This is to be done for three reasons: 1) to un-oppress

a nation by disengaging the governing body from the barbaric ways they live and the people have to live; 2) to have civil peace and share God's good news; and 3) to free up and loosen the money that is not being used to help create a better world.

The money that we are talking about that has been stolen that does not belong to the thief is considered a part of the recompense that belongs to mankind that the spirit of the principles of Satan is holding captive through the mindset of someone that is blind to the fact of reality that it doesn't belong to you in the first place and it is to be used to finance the good doing of the needs of humankind. This is not limited to mankind but animals also.

It is written that the thief must return what belongs to others. It is my faith that this may be one of the ways to get billions released and loose into the world's economy to strengthen it so it might lead to increasing the body of Christ and 100 plus years for the planet earth or mother earth and father time to stay married in the presence of people.

Who are the ones who need a new insurance policy for the coverage of eternal life? Who is responsible for them getting it if not way of me or you then who?

The therapy that we teach others how to apply doesn't start as a place in the conscious state of mind as most psychologists or psychiatrists would have made known the way they consider to create a new way of thinking. The restoration starts in the heart with what could be called the dance of a thousand pricks meaning to touch the heart as many times as need be to change the spirit without a fight.

Think of towerism as someone building a skyscraper. After the building is as high as it will get, the builder of the tower looks for a way to get even higher. This is where tyrants come into play.

The Curse of The Knowledge of Solomon's Riches

This I will refer to as elephantitis or the black elephant curse. This curse has tied a part of the people with an animalist mind and spirit together and won't let them become free to become a blessing with the wealth they control. It is an unknown fact that the billions they are in control of can help to rebuild the world's economy and this could last on a scale of one hundred or more years.

What Can Be Learned

What is the goal? To get people connected to the Holy Spirit. They might not like this because it has a problem with the will of self and it will not fight with it but mankind will fight with themselves and until they are done the holy spirit won't come in to help guide and redirect a person in the right direction if they need it. That is the job we can help do for someone at BTHPM. The patterns of being troubled are all the same they may have developed in all kinds of ways but to come out of the self-denial of getting the right kind of help you need them applying it to your life comes by one way or from one way, change and the best start from the bottom up in one way but the top down work on ok! The explosion is there because when someone hits bottom they will listen but when they are on top they may not.

Now the process or steps we at BTHPM use is the bottom up to get the cream of the crop to rise to the top to see the grave as a place of rest gives the departure of their one way will not be any more darkness in the figure of speaking on the level of getting connected with the right source of income that will supply you with all of your needs on the one fact that most people don't get straight the fact of the things they really don't need. We have become a people that have no need of too many needs we have that is damaged our life and the planting also the greed that some have that need to be fixed in their heart. This is a mission that will take this work around the world and back again to create new ways of life for millions of people that will make the world smile.

I do hope that the way we are growing is the best way possible to add to the foundation of unfolding the answers that may seem a mystery to others. As far as us this can and will be done through the kingdom building process that is being done as the heavenly father sees fit. Now have you been chosen to help this process on a financial level and I am thankful to you for whatever you do to share in this process of growth.

God gives certain privileges to people; it is my hope that we can share the one that never abuses the other, which is love.

Not an order but in order for you to have the concept of this work you will need to have a supernatural level of thought.

Goal

24

The plan is to reach as many oppressed people as possible by first reaching the leaders of the countries that are governed by tyrants and dictators. These tyrants and dictators control all or most of their countries' finances and keep the people oppressed by limiting the resources made available to them.

Tyranny must be eliminated in order for all people to be free. We must reach outside of the comfort of our country in order to help free those who are still oppressed all over the world.

If we reach the leaders, we help the people. It is time to be our brothers' keepers and stop this oppression.

The plan is to get these people exposed to the dance of the love to prick the hearts, nothing more or less. With the information that gives the light of rebirth in the fastest way to create change that is on the spiritual level that can place the mindset on the new level that helps fix the subconscious on an internal level that needs fixing also. God will do the rest.

Leaders: Don't Fear Love

It feels so good to be in the center fuse of the development of a new level of life that is giving an adrenalin rush that sends you somewhat out of this world. This is a known and not shared affect some would compare to the seal of spiritual growth.

Daily I press toward the mark of the excellence in Christ Jesus saying hallelujah!

Then know that you know how safe you are to help keep the blood blue by not spilling a drop!

Now the problem comes in and starts to grow when the unwise pick up a shield and think it is the right one and start to use it against others that means them no harm so they feel like they are right and are wrong as hell and not know this can send them to hell. They are fighting with themselves and others that try to help them and become trapped on a level that all can see but they are blind and at the time seemingly hopeless.

Now what does the possession of the wrong kind of shield mean? You are at war and fighting the wrong ways of life you fight yourself you fight the system to stay alive with greed the way you feel you need to by stealing, lying, cheating and anything that is contrary to the right way in other words backwards. What causes this first not knowing "no" and the partners he has that set you up to produce the okie doke. What do I mean? The thought of being good that we all have because it is an instinct so we use this state of life to get lost in instead of saying "no I won't take advantage of a person's shortcomings just because I can".

If you know what I am saying then you won't have a problem with this, the fact of fear overruling the good in you that won't let go. Well the shield of ungodliness is what holds back millions of people that they won't let go that stop their breakthrough that comes from the lord. The fear of becoming somewhat powerless over what the devil's advocate that is always in the way of the progress on any given time that is the big hold on them now what can be done about it that is personal and it requires the personal relationship with the lord and it is or seems like too much for some to do because of the problem. The aura is unhealthy that gives a sick feeling through the pocket may be fat.

Now for them all I can say is they have not let the ungodly shield go and it is a shame because the Lord wants to use them in ways they may never know.

As for them they think they have the armor of god on and behind their back they have the dark side of themselves that is reflected every time they put up the shield that shows the reflection of something ugly. That is why you have not arrived where you need to be or want to be. That is also why some people have backward thinking that stinks. It is time to get freedom from all that is blinding you.

Now as for those that don't have the godliness they need to do the right thing it has shown through what has been done one big example the games, wars that the people with the wrong shield had that got caught up and fell down in the sea of blood that runs red throughout the country that hide behind them and what happens is the reaction of what they put out harm in most cases the youth of the world. They don't kill themselves all the time the people that sit in high places do it by taking their blessings and hoard or squander it or throw it away. This can stop the power of love is it at hand if you will just join in with one thing the right heart it will guide the mind.

Time to Line Up

What goes on the outline? First what do you have to work with? That is when they need God because mankind can't help in this stage of someone life and they are not blessed if they don't lose their mind because they are already acting somewhat crazy.

Where do we meet in the center? It is called the "lack of actions before knowledge." This came to birth the creation of the new knowledge to unseal the Old Testament way of thinking to a greater way to give us to the New Testament way of thinking in the name of Jesus.

What Is Wrong

I am mostly talking about the people that do the right things for the wrong reasons. Now if you turn this around does it mean the same thing? The answer is to stop; just stop. You can do the right thing for the right reason; all day long!

Change the Darkness That You Can See

Did He? He Did!

Did the Lord prepare him even though Cain killed Abel; you are Abel to set yourself free from the darkness. He died to live for us; it is my belief that he took on the slaying to show others the way to salvation also as others have done.

Now who or what is the biggest demon that has the use of the talent that makes them money? They rain supreme and that support the basis of their position that wreaks havoc on themselves and may destroy them if they don't stop or get the help they need.

This is the demon logic that takes some people to a place where they get lost that causes division in oneself. This phase of division that divided a person up from themselves to cause them to lose sight can be fixed with the lord by them going to him for help. It is the way I know to go. I know no other.

The problem with this level of growth is there is no proper growth in their spirit which creates a shield. This shield locks in the devil's truth and keeps out the good news which leads to freedom. If you are not aware you remain trapped, thirsting for power that can only be quenched from seeing and or creating the flames from fires that look like a good light but are not. The shield was developed through the hardening of the heart. It is time to put out this kind of flames with the Lord's help.

The shield gave people a blind spot that caused you to believe that it can protect you and the only thing that it is doing is stealing time; time to get rid of this problem that you pick up. It is time to learn that it all belongs to God not us. Think about it he created it. Forgive me it is a real no brainer. What may be the biggest factor that makes people act this way is fear of the fact that we are a slave to the development of our life and to combat this we as humans counteract by picking up the invisible shield that Satan puts in front of us not knowing the problem it can and will create one thing when you are a child playing and other children are playing you may grab it to protect yourself. That is where it may have a chance to get stuck to you not knowing that you are playing with fire that wants to burn everyone.

That is why it is our job to protect the children and train them up in the word because if they go astray they can come back home and that is where their heart is at or supposed to be with the Lord. Amen.

The secret wars are coming to an end this veil of secrecy has been seen after more than 2,000 years. How did the level attack people it has been revealed on the personal level that the prince of darkness did this in different ways? One of the biggest ways was they created the invisible shield that appears in man's mind was when Cain killed Abel. Abel was able to stop Cain but he believed he would cut his love off of the time he had to live.

The prince of darkness stepped in the mindset of people and said protect yourself from the bad people if you know better. So this shield was created and Satan developed the concept of the misuse of it.

The people not knowing what they had started killing each other trying to act and think they are right. Then the blind led the blind with the devil leading people shield was born out of Eve. Abel didn't put on a shield and the people they now have fear to not carry one. But like it said it is the wrong kind of shield. It belongs to Satan. It is time to put it down and put on the right kind of armor that the Lord gives us.

The fact that some people hid the one shield behind their back and claim they have the armor of the Lord offends the Lord beware also though they think they can hide behind a big house or car, clothes, jewelry, etc. Don't let this keep you trapped like a dirty rat because it can; it is not worth it.

The real playmate shield for kids of all ages that have a goat's mentality. This is a part of the hidden knowledge that is about you that you are scared to reveal to yourself; you do not want to know it. Now the bigger the shield the more you are revealed; example, guns, knives, weapons and things that do harm to others are a part of this shield. Those that are in gangs and warfare where people create coos again, uprisings, hostage takeovers or rulers that have to kill the people they lead and chooses to harm others that are innocent need to understand this intervention. Now there are the senseless killings that are never seen but does harm also.

Drop the shields before the blood spills to put down the grim reaper, dropping it like it is hot. Unhook yourself from the crook in you. Quit stealing from yourself with the use of this real news and empower yourself.

We are in need of logic and reasoning to create understanding of what is real or not. It is as simple as that.

The one with the thought of living by the gun is the one that carries a shield of steel with bullets working the wrong ways the wrong way.

Let's take it a step further if all the people we know dropped down this ungodly shield on the earth's floor under us would be a walkway again as it was before the fall also in a sense of presence; then as before we have the spirit of mankind that could then lead the new veil of peace because both hands would be free and not carrying the invisible shield of death and destruction that came about from one brother killing another.

This war has now come to pass to do one thing and that is to over mind hell of the people that may be on the road going there.

The Children of the Lord
Are Stopping the Progress of Satan

By not dedicating one's self to a hell sentence and a jail would be better.

Getting back to the state of the world and the people who are to be the leaders and putting American president Donald Trump and the one thing he said is making America first. There is no problem with that if he intends to do that which falls in line with what the Lord wants him to do to help lead us as a people in the USA.

Now I say this because all people are first in the eyes of the Lord in all nations if they obey the calling of who is on first in the body of Christ in the ways he wants them to be. So do we help him know this or do we sit back and say he is supposed to know this for himself? Well, if it is left up to me, the leader needs to learn this from his people if there is a chance he may not know. Therefore, keep it real.

Not to cut the issue short but we have been over it already. What may be the bigger problem a towerist has along with that I have explained in past books they are afraid of the red label of coming down to earth they have fear of being as a common man in a way they fear the blood shedding that happens in the common man's life and the pain of growing. It goes deeper into a lovelessness of not wanting to think of the fact of have a Lord who was beaten and bruised in a way that may frighten the hell out of them in one way be kept it in them in another?

Now how can this be through the illusion of darkness that comes to some people as light that they will do whatever to keep shining bright even if it unknowingly blinds them to a reality that harms others and eventually harms them in the end.

That is why the Lord gives the way up out of a poverty that is known but not known the riches of the world that traps some people is a worse off state of life than some people who have nothing is a death sentence that is waiting to be carried out.

Now not all with the trapping of wealth but if there be one it is too many because the one may harm many. Therefore, it is time to put a stop to this way of allowing sadness and madness to offend the innocence of people of the world. If you don't know where it is at after today then do your homework.

Now off the cuff could the towerism be in a particular country because of the towerism we have in the world?

How to lose the stress about the future of America and this is not fake news

We always live with less when we are spiritually blinded.

This comes from my heart. It may only be my faith and belief that the under-developed countries of the world have a better chance to become more blessed than the developed countries in the world.

This is a real attack on Satan's principles to keep them on a non-existing level of having no effect on human's existence to stop them from growing by way of governing their lives.

As I have written before, I had to be present in Satan's camp on a spiritual quest to learn about the tools to use against his will in mankind to foil his plans to harm people. I was able to make the great escape to the home inside of my heart where the Lord was waiting for my return.

Know that you cannot fight for what is right if you do not know what is wrong

With the possible fry-day you have coming with no more burdens in your future

Welcome

Flying the friendly skies of the spiritual wealth that is needed to help end tyranny all over the world.

People please this is not an illusion. It is a real force of gravity to take you upwards in your mind's eye. If there is a solution to a problem, we can find it and make use of it. Thank you.

No man has had a better answer to a problem than the Lord's wisdom

I always knew that I missed out on a lot but how I knew was by the fight that I had fought.

We can throw legal punches at a leader on a spiritual level.

Get a new scope on the towers with love

Become a fool for the Lord. You will come out wiser

One of the greatest levels of understanding this can be found in a poem called "If" by Rudyard Kipling to place yourself on the Lord's team. It is all about one of my experiences. Anyone in a tower needs to read and live that poem to be a fool for the Lord.

How many need to work out of a problem from the top once you are trapped there? Who needs to go from the bottom up? I cannot really say. We all have to make our own decisions and the Lord's leading a way for them to go.

How many of the world's leaders are cursed by the essence of the spiritual principles? It may be more than we think.

This book is an extension of ending towerism around the world that deals with its extended family of dictatorship, etc. The bottom line is the haters of it that are terrorists because without towerists there would not be terrorists who feel threatened by them on more than one level or they promote both.

We know that we are different and have different issues that we have to handle with our thinking process whether democrat, republican, liberal, green party, etc. Can we all stand under an umbrella of justice for all in order to stop the rain that falls which causes tears of pain instead of tears of joy?

Now to look at it closer, the darkness from the shadows from towers blinds the wisdom that may come from the spiritual factor of a terrorist that led them to a lost generation that believes they will stop darkness that they are shadowed by, by creating more darkness. They see no way to stop it because it does not have an explanation. Thank God there is an explanation. To free one's thinking and show the way up to know of the light means no more fear of the unknown that showed up in the light of day with war because of the spiritual war that Satan has had so many people locked in that is now unlocked for the people to know and show the truth about the misunderstanding of this matter. Fight no more it is time to end this kind of war.

We must give this war back to the Lord to end it. We are to be fixing the ungodliness of this kind of problem by way of the Lord. Satan has tricked us long enough and it is time for us to stop him. The main reason why we are to get ready for the war of all wars is referred to as Armageddon. This will take place and we can be more than prepared by not getting involved with man-made problems that we can eliminate by being on the Lord's side as the real deal to come to earth.

Warning: as it was once before, it will come to pass again for anyone that is wrong in their warring presence will destroy themselves.

Let's take someone in history: if he and we knew about the problem he had called towerism and worked his way down and out of it, how much good he could have done. I am talking about Adolph Hitler. With his tenacity we can turn mountains into molehills.

Time to get over being under siege
Will you be a part of this rebirth?

Even though our higher power has always has a way to give his people a way out, if they don't know they stay there for years such as when Moses led people and they wandered in the wilderness for 40 years. The Lord had presented a plan for and to his people but they were disobedient refer to Numbers 32:13.

Everyone Shout "Give Self a Chance"

Pray for the time to enjoy the calm after the storm once our task is completed. We don't do this to let the four-year task of someone turn into a forty-year sentence of a hellish presence that could be left for someone else to deal with. That someone else is us so do not put the blame on the Trump because God trumps everything with his will and wisdom.

This book is designed to connect you to a level of learning to not deny yourself the wisdom of life as some do. Living with less doesn't mean poverty when the prosperity that you can develop that is exists in heaven, is all that will really matter in life.

Do people want to be subdued with paper love?

We can all create love with our inner potential.

This is a way to look at a nation's leader without deceitfulness or anger that can or will create the right kind of change.

It is nice to know when you talk to a man about himself he will listen for quite a while.

God can turn something we think is bad really bad into good.

We can't let one man, or more, try to steal the joy of a part of your nation.

"towerectomy" – the process of eliminating towerism in someone.

President of Gambia (country in West Africa) lost election March 2017, after 20 years of dictatorship. He was forced to step down. We must do all we can, in a peaceful way, to not allow any leader to oppress people for so long. Now the movement is set for us to see how the elimination of towerism is possible all over the world.

Admit to towerism and come out of the clouds of the elements of the mind and atmosphere of the so-called protection that sin gives to people to a space that will not harm you that confronts the sin and not feel like you will take a stripping in a way that can hurt you because some towerists fear they will have a free fall into a hellish place in their life or be subject to poverty and or are scared of not being powerful and become powerless.

This doesn't have to be because the Lord has a safety net to catch you and the higher you are whether higher than towerism as a dictator or tyrant, etc. The communist state of life that people have to live under can end in this lifetime.

The biggest problem with those in towers of all kinds is to back down from themselves. They have been so intertwined with their earthly properties they fear the thought of ashes to dust that they came from so they think their ego will sustain them for an eternity. It won't last forever and the part in them that they say you must go back to a child has presented itself in a way that has locked them into a state that has shown up as a place that is harmful and they refuse to deal with it consciously. That allows it to defraud them and it becomes selfish and drowns them with the fact of air they breathe not knowing one day they will not sustain their life off of air but love and love alone.

The people who persevere to deceive themselves can become free once again as it was meant to be at their birth. Amen

This book was created to help join the people of the world together in more unity in order to free the unclean spirits and increase the economy with the wealth that is not being used to bring about a new income level where there is none for the people to have their needs met; sharing of wealth that can only indicate love.

This book or message was not written to change the leaders of the different countries in the world but to change their attitudes about the ways they are governing the people and policies they are somewhat locked into too give them a way to understand if they have a personal problem that affect the multitude of people who want to look up to them in a good way so they can admit to the wrong thing you have been doing to a higher power and even if you don't admit it to the people show them you are mending your ways.

The message is to not create a (coup) or create a takeover by the people who may be living in poverty. It is to create a seen fire of negative energy that has come between the people and the leader of each and every nation on the earth within the ranks of what has been made right and wrong to see the ways of good and evil to change the hand that rules man by man into a hand that is ruled by the Lord by way of mankind and kindness more so than anything else in life.

Now learn to let not the opposite curse of someone be upon your presence as a ruler. Because this is the reversal of the Solomon curse that has fell upon some of mankind.

Now, Patience is a Virtue!

Isaiah 40:31

Learn how to pass out of the past to live in the present of the youth future so the seeds are some to outgrow our foolishness.

Sometimes we have to remember when it is time to back track on someone's writing from the past to know what can be a part of your future. When it comes down to the return things right again thank you present.

Who will be the pied piper of the nation you live in the already leader or you?

Believe

There is no sense of hopelessness or helplessness in our world!

Holy Spirit

It is nice to know of someone who thinks better than me who thinks their thoughts our through me to show other people.

Let it be known it is not us waiting for the Lord it is the Lord waiting for us to do the will he has set into action for us that we have been blessed with. That is why we must move forward in stopping tyranny in the world. To enable the Lord to do his work we must do ours. The process of ending poverty comes from having spiritual sight that eliminates poverty from the sight and out of peoples' lives. It may not come in the way we may want it to all the time but it shows up on time and in time and provides the sustenance and nourishment; no buts about it; what a way out of what looks like no way. To God all lives matter.

Take Note

Everyone involved should be even more proud of themselves in their presence of changing the course of their nations' history.

The book is designed to connect people to a level of learning which will help light up the darkness that may be in and/or around them. The darkness causes some people to deny wisdom to enhance life. Living with less doesn't mean living in poverty. The prosperity that can be developed lies in heaven and that is all that really matters in life.

To The People

Know that you can't make people do the right thing, because of free will. Each person must do it for themselves.

Muse-News

God doesn't need help taking troublemakers off the table it is up to you now!

The Real News

Even though the downfall is inevitable, there are always new towers trying to go up.

The explanation of the arrows of prayer is in the book _Calm During the Storm_ that builds a stairway to step down out of the towers and knowing of a safety net that is under us all to catch us. Without it someone could fall into hell because Satan does not supply one. This book will include more of an explanation about towerists along with the book that tells you how to refrain yourself from being a towerist in order to save the headaches that come with all new generations.

The Beginning

What may take place that you can let pass you by? It is the nervous energy. You now have adapted your mind, body and spirit to grow from and not get confused within to end this problem.

Now may be the right time to take a hiatus from yourself to let the thinking in you be done by someone else.

As I said once or more in one of the many books I have authored, it is heavy falling up and only light-weights fall down.

Changing Spirituality
Down but Not Out

Now is the time for the righteous people of the earth to go out with a big bang in the development of the power of love to let Satan know we all stand in united in life and death for the Lord.

We can know that we don't have to live on the edge as we are somewhat doing in the countries of the world because of the indecisiveness of others. If we learn to make the move that we are responsible to do.

Now the book I write time to stop living on the edge will help in doing that but you can and should know about the problems we are facing to put it all together that refer to towerism and how we can help change that. This is because we are supposed to cast our cares and concern to the Lord. It is time to change your attitude from being Boo-boo the foolish.

We all can make our lives like we are only beefing with the devil and he has not the winning presence that the Lord has over use. Now who are the over One hundred plus with in the number who will claim it and will come forth to all of the world and they will let us know who they are that step down out of the tower of the used in a unfaithful power that keep people confused and lost out of touch with the needs of common people in order to reverse a curse to receive the layman touch for others on a godly level.

Do not let the detours become your matter. What did you say? Think now what do you say?

This information I want people to use as an example in order to for see their future in the right way to get there spiritual star that is a guiding light.

We do not throw material stones

If I rise what do I do to help all people rise to know not to throw a stone If I have committed a sin? The unseen stone I throw is to build a mountain with one side that sits on a side of a tower that can be as a stairway so someone can walk down and out of a place they have trapped themselves in.

Now I must know it cannot be seen by the naked eyes because it need not be and what its part of is to allowed a place that can only be walked on by an invisible spirit of darkness that comes out of someone to walk into light then recognize with its self that frees someone out of a dark place they were within one's self; that way people come to a time and pathway through the womb of their spirit to a spiritual rebirth with righteousness.

Now if you do not like the metaphor of stones then out of the love of the father just imagine you are putting another brick in the wall of stairs to help the towerists come down. This is to help people create escapism. Now let the Lord use you even if you have to carry a cross all by yourself at a time in life also pray for the completion of the walk way down.

The book *Calm During the Storm* helps to provide a spirit for others to live by. This may be a way to get president Donald to learn to deal the deals that the Lord can place upon him that the people are waiting for in the USA. It is also with greater hope this book does the same in all other parts of the world!

An Analogy

Life can be like you are a piece of toast. There are some people who think people are like a piece of chocolate and you never know what to expect until you bite into it. I say if you are like toast them once you learn what it is that can burn you change you have the power to pop up to not get fried. Take note: no one likes burnt toast, even if it is French style!

When a Tower Falls

The opposite of la-la land without a curse is, knowing no one's life needs to be put on a life preserver to have to live by. To this kind of presence in anyone's gift. It is time to stop the senselessness that takes away from others who were made subject to surrender under what is not equal because of creating fear that is wrong and backward. It is time to come forward.

Fishing for the souls of mankind takes a pole which has been created by the Lord. He has the hook and line to help you get caught up in his love.

People have no need to excuse themselves from doing what is right. They only have to start working with themselves and this owner's manual that was developed for them. Do you know who if this is what you really need? If not, try it you may learn to love it. Thank you and may the Lord bless you.

Noting

We are looking forward to working with the alliance of people in the different areas of life that has come under the <u>exposure</u> of this book through a new way of development. It is our privilege to help with their transition in any way it needs to give them the best advice or guide them in the right direction with the development of their countries' affairs and finances of a new lifestyle to create a welcoming to democracy or a culture that will serve all of the people no matter where they are in the world.

Welcome all to a new beginning!